We have a lot to talk about...
IT'S CANCER

We have a lot to talk about...
IT'S CANCER

Jordan Spencer

XULON PRESS

Xulon Press
2301 Lucien Way #415
Maitland, FL 32751
407.339.4217
www.xulonpress.com

Unless otherwise indicated, Scripture quotations taken from the
Christian Standard Bible. (CSB). Copyright © 2017 by Holman Bible
Publishers. Used by permission. All rights reserved

Printed in the United States of America.

ISBN-13: 978-1-5456-8151-0

TABLE OF CONTENTS

DEDICATION

I would like to dedicate this book to my wife, Megan Spencer. We do not always choose the easy path, but our life together is so much better because of it. I pray these stories and words will remind you of how much you have accomplished in your life so far and how many people around the world love you, none more than me.

Also, I would like to dedicate this book to my father, Danny Spencer, who taught me to always do the right thing and to take care of my family. I always look up to you and could not be prouder of you in your journey serving the Lord.

I would like to thank my mother, Pam Spencer, for helping me put this story together in a logical form and for all the countless ways you have helped us behind the scenes. Finally, I would like to thank John Kerry, my little brother in TKE. Thank you for giving me the courage to write this book and perhaps tell a story that will provide hope and encourage people to live their best lives.

INTRODUCTION

C ancer does not have to be the end, but the fight against cancer is not easy. It's an everyday fight. We choose to wake up every day, not knowing what the day will bring but with the choice to not live in fear.

This is a story to honor my wife, Megan Spencer. She was diagnosed at twenty-eight years old with stage four breast cancer. For Megan, as well as my family, cancer is not the conclusion of our story; rather, it has given us the opportunity to live. The past three years since her diagnosis were some of the hardest years of our lives, but they were also some of our best. We saw communities of people come together for the common good of a single family. We witnessed an early maturing of our four-year-old little girl who wanted to take the stress and pain off her mother and nurse her back to health. We saw our son grow as a kind, caring, and sensitive little boy who is always looking for a hug or an opportunity to make someone else happy. As a married couple, for the first time since our wedding night, we laughed until we cried. I would never say that cancer is the best thing that has ever happened to us, and we realize that we are blessed, but our eyes are open, and our hearts are full.

Mentally, you can never be prepared to receive a diagnosis like cancer. To me, the mental battles were the hardest part. Not knowing what the future held or the next day could hold was rough. There are small trials that happen daily, and when compounded with larger obstacles, it is easy to become overwhelmed.

Physically, Megan has gone through hell with her body. In spite of hair loss, a port, a double mastectomy, and radiated skin, she has never looked more beautiful. She got tired and nauseated and suffered through unimaginable pain, but she rarely complained.

Spiritually, we have and continue to experience God's grace. God reached down, wrapped His hands around us, took the cancer out of Megan, and gave her incredible strength when we were under attack by forces from the spiritual realm.

God gave us an opportunity to live an excellent life, and we never want to take that for granted again. We wanted to share our story in order to provide hope for people who are going through a chronic illness. Also, there have been so many people that have helped us along the way, some that we know very well and others that to this day, we have never met. This is a small way we can say "thank you" and "we love you," and when a large group of people do a little, the world can change. Here is our story.

CHAPTER 1

HAVING A BLESSED FAMILY

Our Foundation

I am a big fan of reading and listening to podcasts and try to use any opportunity I can find to improve myself. On a podcast I had the pleasure of listening to a short time ago, a great author spoke of living by a code. This speaker used the reference of a very wealthy man who was traveling across the ocean on a big ship. The boat, for whatever reason, sank, and the wealthy man was stranded on an island. Everyone on the boat knew of the man and knew he was carrying something of great value, and the wealthy passenger soon realized he was not alone on the island. The podcast author asked the listener—if you were the wealthy person on the island, who would you want with you? A carpenter? A chef? A wildlife expert? Or would you rather know that the person you are with is a Christian? You understand that by them being Christian, they have committed to live by a certain moral code.

I want to start our story by proclaiming that I am a Christian, and my wife Megan and I try to live our lives in a way that demonstrates Christian values.

We Have a Lot to Talk About

What a loaded statement. This small phrase marked the beginning of a whole new life for my family and me. Now, I will pass this same sentiment to you. This phrase will come up again in the story, but we need to lay a better foundation.

November 2006—School Cafeteria Thanksgiving meals are wonderful; however, that Thursday I was feeling a little sour. The next night was a formal party for my fraternity, and I had yet to secure a date. I was eating with my buddy Greco, and we were both brainstorming on who we knew that would be fun to bring. Next thing I knew, a beautiful brunette walked past and sat by herself a few tables over. I remember jokingly telling Greco, "One day, I'm gonna marry that girl." At that time, it's what most immature, single, overconfident, idiot males would say when a beautiful girl was in sight. I told him with complete confidence that I would get her to go with me to the formal. Greco, being the good friend that he was, encouraged me to give it a try after laughing, which implied that I didn't stand a chance. I walked up to her, and we exchanged pleasantries. She said her name was Megan and that she recognized me as an RA in the dorms. When I asked her to the dance, she gracefully turned me down and said she thought she had plans. I told her to give me her number and that I would call her later to make sure, *wink wink*. She turned down that proposition saying, "Why don't you just give me yours instead?" I knew I was doomed. Later, she educated me on how uncool I was to invite a girl to a formal party the day before and expect her to have a dress and all the fixings.

Being the ultimate pick-up line master of the universe is tough; however, later that same night, it was different. We were both

2

working a fundraiser at a culinary event for school when I noticed her working the dessert station. I was a service captain, so as we were serving, I had to walk past her station frequently. Megan noticed me and smiled a couple of times, but when it came time for me to talk to her, I couldn't. She really took my breath away. I panicked and let out a whistle, the kind of *whew-whew* that Pepé Le Pew would let out on his charades to get the girl. At first, she didn't say anything. She just stood there, and I thought, *Man, I'm an idiot.* Then, she looked at me and said, "Tell me about it, stud." She said it in the same voice as Sandy from the movie *Grease*. We laughed, and I was hooked. We randomly bumped into each other at an after party that night and stayed up all night talking. Finally, we got back to campus as the sun was coming up. As I walked into the dorm, the house mother working the front desk made a sarcastic remark about how happy she was that I'd made it home. I just smiled and kept walking, more like floating on air.

The next week was actual Thanksgiving week, and Megan made it to my hometown of Zachary, Louisiana, to meet my family. The next weekend, I went to Carencro, Louisiana, to meet her family. We hit it off right away, and I am grateful for them.

Growing Stronger in Love

The saying goes, "Absence makes the heart grow fonder." Well, we tested the hell out of that phrase.

In culinary school, we were required to do two externships. The first summer we were together, she moved to Arkansas for three months to live with her brother and work at a restaurant near his house. The next summer, she moved to New York to work at a

3

prestigious country club. That was another three months apart. A year later, I had graduated and decided to go to Florida International University to pursue my master's degree in hospitality and tourism management. I don't want to discount the fact that I can cook, but when it came to working next to Megan or some other folks I have had the pleasure to work with, I am no top chef. I found I was more of an expert in the eating experience, so I wanted to work on more "front of the house" opportunities.

Megan still had another semester, so she had to stay, but we both agreed at the time that it was the best move for my future to go to Florida. (We will talk about out-of-state college tuition later!)

Every minute we spent apart, I missed her like crazy. I knew that she wasn't the kind of person to be held back and that she needed to spread her wings. Honestly, I wasn't sure if we would survive our time apart. I knew I loved her, and she loved me. The first time she told me she loved me was at a Mardi Gras parade after a few beverages. I think it caught both of us off guard, but she blurted it out, and I was completely happy that she did. When Megan decided to move to Florida to be with me, I knew this relationship was something more than usual.

About a month after Megan moved to Florida, it hit me like a ton of bricks. I was sitting on the beach talking to my friend Nancy when it finally became clear that I had to marry Megan. Love wasn't even a question; we were in love. Trust wasn't a question because I trusted her with every part of me and everything I had. Megan was and still is the most beautiful woman I have ever seen. She is sexy and classy with a sense of humor that will bring you to your knees and an independent mindset that doesn't take any crap from anyone. I was hooked, so I did what any young and

4

madly-in-love man would do. I financed a ring! Don't worry—I paid it off with my leftover student loans (not a proud moment). The evening before I popped the question, I called Megan's mother to tell her my plans. She told me how proud she was of Megan for not just being a hard worker but for how good of a person she'd turned out to be. I had a great relationship with her family and was happy to have Megan join mine.

The morning of her birthday, July 28, 2010, I had just gotten home around midnight from working in a restaurant. I couldn't sleep, so I just laid in bed nervously. I was giddy inside. I woke her up around 4:30 am and told her that for her birthday, I wanted to take her to see the sunrise on the beach. Fort Lauderdale is on the east coast of Florida, so you never see the sun go down, but the sunrises there are magnificent. I think part of me was nervous about what she would say, so I figured I would up my chances by catching her off guard before she really woke up. It worked! We sat on top of a picnic bench, and I started telling her all the sappy sayings. Finally, I stood up just as the sun started to crest above the waves, got down on my knee, and asked her to marry me. She cried, pulled me up, and said, "1,000 times, yes!"

It was a quiet, intimate moment and one of the most special times of my life that I will cherish always. I took her to the Miami aquarium that day. I was exhausted, but I didn't care; I was in love.

A couple years later, I graduated from Florida International University and was a restaurant manager at one of the largest restaurants in Miami. We sat 800 people, had 2 bars—1 inside and 1 outside—a pool, and a dock since we were right on the water. Half of my day was spent watching yachts, managing crazy pool parties with guest DJ's, and keeping sports fans happy with the

120 big screen TVs and many projector screens. We were always busy, and I loved it.

At that same time, Megan had worked up to being a supervisor at one of the most beautiful Marriot resorts in the world, the Marriott Harbor Beach in Fort Lauderdale, Florida. She worked with an amazing team and did some exciting things there.

We worked a lot, but we didn't care. We were able to ride our bikes to the beach, and we lived very simply in the two-room hut we rented behind someone else's house.

It's Wedding Season

We got married on 6/11/11—a date handpicked by me so it would be easy to remember. The week before the wedding, some of my best friends started to arrive in Louisiana for the festivities. One of them, Darren "Boomadang" Warren, showed up with a rattail. Megan made him shave it off if he wanted to be in the wedding. She gave it back to Darren, who kept it, and when it came time for him to get married, he gave the rattail back to us in a frame.

On the day of the wedding, I was checking into the hotel, the luxurious Days Inn, and ended up in the elevator <u>alone</u> with Megan's grandfather. He looked at me and said, "You know this shit is forever right?"

6

He was one of the kindest gentlemen I have ever met. But, as with a lot of older, wiser men, he had a way of looking you in the eye and, without saying much, striking the fear of God in you.

We held the wedding at an old plantation house right outside of Lafayette, Louisiana. The ceremony was set up on the front lawn. It was a beautiful setting outside at sunset; however, thirty minutes before the ceremony, the bottom fell out. The staff scrambled to move all the chairs inside and out of the rain. We ended up inside the plantation, and half of our audience had to stand around a balcony overlooking the ceremony. In her vows, Megan said she loved me and promised to always, no matter what. In my vows, I told her I loved her more than all the spicy chicken sandwiches in the world. We also promised to love each other in sickness and in health. At that time, I don't think we fully understood what that meant. However, we would receive a lesson on it before long.

Broke and Babies

One morning, Megan woke me up after I had worked late at the restaurant. I was a little aggravated, but then I noticed the pair of baby shoes on the bed next to me. My heart sank, and I said, "What is that for?" I knew what those shoes meant, but I was in shock.

She said, "You are going to have some big shoes to fill!" She was so excited, but I was terrified.

Megan was offered a position at the Marriott Vanderbilt in Nashville, Tennessee. We decided that South Florida was fun but we wanted to settle down a bit, and moving to Tennessee was just what we needed. We loaded up a U-Haul and moved out that way. We decided to move near our relatives in Murfreesboro, Tennessee, and commute to Nashville. As irony would strike, the hotel that Megan got hired at needed a food and beverage supervisor, so we got to work together on occasion.

I asked Megan one time toward the end of her pregnancy, "When are you going to stop working?"

She basically asked right back, "Why would I stop working?" To me, it was obvious; however, I had to ask in the least sarcastic way possible. "Because you are starting to get a little round, and this job requires you to be on your feet all day, holding sharp things, and being under a significant amount of stress, etc."

She just smiled and asked, "So you think I look fat?" Dang, I walked right into that one! Sure enough, Megan worked up until she went into labor, and Kinley came late.

When Megan finally went into labor, she chose a natural birth. She didn't take a drop of medicine. She labored for twelve hours, and finally, they broke her water to help speed up the process. We were finally parents—broke but completely whole.

It might seem like a good gig working in a hotel, but being in the lower level-management side just wasn't lucrative. Megan breastfed, which helped a lot financially and is supposed to help prevent breast cancer, right? We couldn't afford daycare, so Megan would go in around 5:00 am and work breakfast and lunch. When she would come home around 2:00 pm, I would leave around 3:00 pm after handing off the baby and work until 2:00 am. It was a miserable time in our lives. If we got three hours of sleep in a row, we were lucky. Kinley was a good baby, but she didn't care much for sleep. On the few days we had off together, one of us would take Kinley somewhere so that the other could get some sleep. This went on for about six months until Megan got the opportunity to become the executive chef for the Doubletree Hilton in Murfreesboro, Tennessee. Shortly after that, I received the opportunity to become the purchasing manager at the third largest hotel in Nashville. These opportunities came with more stable hours and a little more pay, which allowed for us to give that extra money to a daycare. My mother-in-law decided on a change and moved to Tennessee to be near us, which was awesome and helped a lot. Everything seemed to be falling into place, but after some long conversations and Kinley turned one, we decided it was time to head on home to Louisiana.

Megan had an opportunity to work for Sysco Foods, and I was going to go work in my family's business. Our son Cohen was born not too long after this, and the only difference was Megan being in natural labor for a cool twenty-eight hours.

9

The Fighter

I want to shed a little light on Megan as she is extraordinary. While we were living in Florida, she was invited to be the vacation chef for Vice- President Joe Biden and his wife Jill. One of Megan's repeat customers in Florida was friends with the VP and very wealthy. He owned a huge house in the Keys and invited Joe to come on vacation. After background checks and interrogations by the Secret Service, she was all set—twenty-one years old and the private chef for one of the most powerful men in the world!

As I said before, by age twenty-four, she was the executive chef for a major hotel chain, Doubletree by Hilton, where she was in charge of a restaurant, banquets, room service, etc., all while she had a one-year-old at home.

She took a job with Sysco Foods after we decided to change our paths so we could spend more time with our growing family. She never sold a stick of gum professionally, and after her first year, she won "Rookie-of-the-Year."

There is a lot to say about someone as talented and motivated as Megan. As her husband, I am her biggest cheerleader. Moreover, I would like to add that Megan is kind. She is a good person that loves her family, friends, and, most importantly, the Lord. Love never fails.

CHAPTER 2

WE HAVE A LOT TO TALK ABOUT

Psalm 23
The Good Shepherd
A Psalm of David.

¹The LORD is my shepherd;
I have what I need.
²He lets me lie down in green pastures;
he leads me beside quiet waters.
³He renews my life;
he leads me along the right paths
for his name's sake.
⁴Even when I go through the darkest valley,
I fear no danger,
for you are with me;
your rod and your staff — they comfort me.
⁵You prepare a table before me
in the presence of my enemies;
you anoint my head with oil;
my cup overflows.
⁶Only goodness and faithful love will pursue me

all the days of my life,
and I will dwell in the house of the LORD
as long as I live.

I was sitting in church one Sunday in the fall of 2015 when my pastor was preaching on loving the Lord no matter what happens. I remember him saying, "Bad things are going to happen," and it was like everything got quiet. I heard a voice on the inside saying, "Something is coming up, and it's going to be hard, but I need you to get through it to get to where I need you to be. It will involve Megan."

I believe that God speaks to us in many ways. This was the first time I had ever heard a voice, although it wasn't audible. My incredible pastor was preaching another Sunday morning a year or so before this, and he was talking about how we are stewards for God's stuff and that it all belongs to Him, so we better take care of it. For example, he mentioned that he keeps his lawnmower clean because it is God's. This was interesting because the day before, my riding lawnmower had just randomly died in the yard. I was certain it had to do with the fuel line, but there was nothing I could do to get it running.

After that service, I went home and could not get it going again. I sat there and remembered church, so I prayed, "God, this is your lawnmower. Let's get it running." I turned the key, and nothing happened. I got frustrated at this point and kind of angrily said, "God, I just need that SPARK!" The same scenario occurred, where everything got quiet, and I got a chill. I randomly, or not so randomly, had the thought that I should check the spark plug. The cap had popped off, so, smiling at my own stupidity, I popped it back on. The lawnmower cranked right up and ran like a champ. After that, I cleaned that lawnmower up, washing every detail. I had to keep God's lawnmower clean.

Back in church, I heard the familiar voice, but this time it was a little vaguer. The following January of 2016, we were coming home from the airport after being in New York City for my birthday. We were in separate cars, and Megan was in front of me. A man ran a red light and T-boned Megan. She had a couple broken ribs and a totaled car, but she was okay. I remembered the voice and thought, *Okay, we made it*. However, this was just the beginning of a rough year.

Dr. Appointment

It was a Wednesday around lunch time when I received a call from Megan. I was at a local burger joint when she called and invited me to her doctor's appointment. She said she had taken a test and was getting the results today. I nonchalantly said okay and that I could move my schedule around a bit. I met her there approximately thirty minutes later and sat in the waiting room. I needed to go to the restroom, so I went through the door past the receptionist to the back. When I finished and was walking back, I came around the corner, and a doctor ran smack into me and dropped a stack of papers. Clearly, she was distracted and troubled but gave me a brief smile. Little did I know that a few minutes later, we would be sitting in that doctor's examination room.

It was a typical examination room at a doctor's office. Megan was sitting on the examination bed, and I in the corner chair. We were cutting up as usual when the doctor walked in. She closed the door and recognized me from the hall, apologizing again for bumping into me. I laughed and said it was no big deal, and the consult began. The words I will never forget came out: *"We have a lot to talk about Megan; you have cancer."* The doctor continued to explain that they had sent the biopsy tissue off to the lab and it had come back positive. When the words came out of her mouth, I felt like I had been punched in the stomach. I couldn't talk, and I started wearing out the tissues. An abstract drawing of a garden hung on the wall in front of me. It gave out the vibe that "life is beautiful." I hated that picture. I looked over at Megan, and she just had this blank stare on her face. She looked down, and the doctor asked if she could get her anything. Megan said, "No, I just need a minute." The room was quiet for a good twenty seconds, and suddenly, Megan looked up and set the tone for the future. She said, "Okay, just tell me what I need to do." She never cried, showed fear, or gave any indication of the weight of her situation. It's like she saw this as an opportunity or just something else to put on her plate, like us moving to a new house or having another kid. It seemed like she was thinking, *Just give me the instruction pamphlet and let me know what steps to take!*

The doctor had more of my approach. She looked terrified and rehearsed; moreover, I couldn't imagine being in her shoes. Having to be the one to tell a twenty-eight-year-old mother that she has cancer in multiple spots in her body and explain the outlook is not as systematic and fluid as it is in the movies. She explained that with the lack of family history, how quickly it had spread, and it's occurrence at such a young age that some immediate actions needed to be taken. However, not knowing how far and where it had spread was one of the most frustrating parts. I remember asking a generic question along the lines of, "Is she going to be okay?"

The doctor gave a spine-tingling answer of, "We are going to do everything we can to make sure she will be." But God...

After receiving a little more instruction on how to move forward, we finally left. We walked down the hall in a daze. I eventually said, "What in hell just happened?"

Megan said, "We are just going to have to figure it out." She was comforting me! She said, "Let's try to get out of here before the traffic gets bad." Yeah, like that's what I was worried about! We were in separate cars, and I told her I needed to take a drive. Megan said she would get the kids and meet me at the house.

Besides the initial shock of the announcement from the doctor, I think, outwardly, I held it together well. But I knew I had to go tell the one person I always went to when there was a problem (or I was in trouble), my father.

I drove to his office after confirming he was there. I walked in, and he was visiting with my Aunt KK. My dad looked at me and said, "Jordan, what's going on?" I guess he could read my face better than anyone. I couldn't answer and just stared. He said, "Oh no, it's bad isn't it!" I nodded my head and began to sob, still not able to talk. My aunt made the implication that she would leave and give us some space, but I said no, that I wanted her to stay. I managed to squeeze out "Megan...cancer." He got up from behind his desk and gave me that comforting hug only a parent can give. Eventually, we sat back down and began to talk it out. I did feel better once I got the news off my chest. I knew in my head I needed my dad in our corner, and he was there with flying colors.

15

Later that night, we had a lot to talk about, but Megan and I could barely talk. We did a great job at dinner with the kids keeping the conversation normal. Once able to lay in bed, there was nervous tension in the room. I panicked a little and consequently said an inappropriate joke. It went along the lines of that for Halloween, I would dress up like Dr. Evil, and Megan would be the bald, wrinkled cat that would sit next to me, and I would just pet her. I figured that by Halloween, she would be bald. Still a bad joke, but she loved it! She started laughing out loud, and for the first time in a long time, we laughed until we cried. We decided that night, mere hours from hearing the diagnosis, that we would not let our situation affect our family in a negative way and would make the best out of every situation. There would be plenty foot-in-mouth moments, but this was the moment we had a choice and could decide our outcome in accordance with God's plan for us. We chose to laugh.

A few days after this, Megan told me what she wanted for her birthday. She wanted to have family pictures made to remember what we were like before she went through chemo, etc., and wanted the kids to see her how she was. I wasn't very excited about the idea as I was yet to accept the reality of what was going on. I didn't want a great memory of her; I wanted her. I want my wife how she is today and any way she will be in the future. Get behind me, Satan! But as usual, the lady got her way, and the pictures were truly amazing. When we took the pictures, our friend Theresa was able to capture the love we shared together. Now, I am glad we have them as it shows how far we have come.

Test Yo' self Before You Wreck Yo' self

Let's back up a few months, around the time of Megan's car wreck. She had a procedure that some ladies get when their children suck the life out of their breasts, and she wasn't happy with the deflation. Before the surgery, she felt a little lump on the bottom of her right breast. She didn't think too much of it, and when she met with her doctor, he said she shouldn't worry about it.

A few weeks later on the day of the surgery, the lump was still there, and she brought it up again. He said it was probably just a cyst and that it wasn't that big of a deal. The doctor went ahead with the surgery.

A few weeks later, the lump had grown, and the implant really pushed it out. It was approximately the size of a ping pong ball by then. When she went back for a follow-up, she was told that it was probably just a calcium deposit and that it should go away. She was under the impression that because of her age and health, it wasn't a big deal and would go away on its own.

Fast forward a couple of months—she had now asked on multiple occasions the doctor's opinion on something that might not have been serious but should have been taken way more seriously. Spiritually, do you think the devil, the great deceiver, had a hand in this? He put out his best work on Megan, and she was under attack. Even I was so blind and never would have imagined anything like this would happen to Megan. I admit that when she talked to me about it, I downplayed the situation, being ignorant of the possibilities. At this point, the lump(s) never seemed to get better. Megan went in for the final consult with the plastic surgeon, which lasted about a minute, and he said, "You are good to go."

She asked him, "What about these lumps in my breast?"

He looked at them and brought his partner in, and they said, "Maybe you should get that looked at."

She went to another doctor, who immediately was not impressed by the look of Megan's breast and ordered a scan and then a biopsy. This was the test result that led to, "We have a lot to talk about."

If you are like me, looking back, I am pissed at that doctor. I will not give any further details as we signed a non-disclosure agreement. That agreement gave us our money back, and we hope gave that doctor a wake-up call. After prayer and counsel, we could have filed legal actions, but it could have been a drawn-out, ugly process with no guarantee. I wanted Megan to focus on fighting cancer. At that time, we had no assurances on the outcome, and I could not fathom Megan spending her precious time going to court.

I realize now why I see so many commercials saying to get yourself checked and that "Early detection is the best prevention." If Megan would have gotten a biopsy or have been diagnosed at the very beginning, it would have changed a lot of things. We would have been looking at stage one or two cancer, not stage three or four. These days, if you catch the cancer early enough, you take some pills, and it's such a minor process compared to what we were looking at. I was one of those men that would downplay every-thing and go to the doctor only when necessary — not anymore. You know someone with cancer and have more than likely thought about them on occasion while reading our story. I am going to try to steer clear of statistics relating to cancer and how over a million people are diagnosed each year, almost two million. Pray for them to find God's grace because if you are fighting the devil and a killer disease, you want the ultimate Healer and Physician to cover you.

One of Megan's doctors, Dr. Hannaman, was one of the greatest support systems we had. Can you imagine a doctor that cared for his patients enough to give them his personal cell phone number to call any time they had a question or concern? Not just that, but he answered. This part of the story made Dr. Hannaman furious, the neglect that was shown. There was a piece of legislation he was trying to get fixed that would help stop these situations and better protect patients. He said he knew Megan couldn't talk spe-cifics but asked if she would testify before the Louisiana legisla-tors and tell her story, without calling out any details. The state of Louisiana allows doctors to say that they are board-certified without stating by which board. For example, if you are a podiatrist, you can decide to go into plastic surgery and claim to be a board-certified doctor, albeit not certified in plastic surgery—just certified to check out feet. Our doctor said that although we had signed the non-disclosure, we could still help keep others from going through the same situation. Megan is not a public speaker, so it surprised me very much when she said yes. Megan ended up sending a video testimony to the legislators, and it did help them change the law!

When I think back on the courage it would take to stand before Louisiana's lawmakers and tell your story that could impact the passing of a bill, I am still inspired by Megan's stregnth. Dr. Hanneman is a gentleman. I pray one day I can help others the way he helped us.

CHAPTER 3

THE LULL

1 Corinthians 13:4-8

4 Love is patient, love is kind. It does not envy, it does not boast, it is not proud.
5 It does not dishonor others, it is not self-seeking, it is not easily angered, it keeps no record of wrongs.
6 Love does not delight in evil but rejoices with the truth.
7 It always protects, always trusts, always hopes, always perseveres.
8 Love never fails. But where there are prophecies, they will cease; where there are tongues, they will be stilled; where there is knowledge, it will pass away.

None of us will be in this skin and bones forever. We all know where trains start and stop if there is only one track. We all know that if you boil water, it is hot. We all know that if your kids are playing with Legos on the floor, they will not pick them all up, and you will eventually step on one.

Everyone that has experienced being diagnosed with cancer knows that the doctor tells you that you have cancer, but initially, they <u>don't know</u> exactly what/where/how much, etc. To me, this was a tough time, the not knowing. The picture of the doctor's face told a sad story, but who knows, maybe it would turn out differently. Recently, a friend of mine's wife was diagnosed with breast cancer. It looked like they had caught it early; however, in the beginning, the doctors told them they thought they saw a spot on a vital organ. If we are all God-fearing Christians, we should not worry about our lives here on earth, except to serve the Lord and follow Jesus. However, one of the cruelest parts of the journey was given to that couple. For a matter of a few days, they had to wonder if that small spot could mean a much worse prognosis, the worst outcome. The devil loves this time and uses it to plant seeds of fear and worry. During this lull in our story, Megan and I did something a little less orthodox. The day after we were told she was carrying cancer in her body; we went to Florida to party!

This picture was taken right when we arrived in Florida. It's hard for the common eye to tell that twenty-four hours before we were in the doctor's office getting diagnosed with cancer. I can tell by my eyes I didn't get much sleep, but I was determined to make sure Megan had a great time.

Megan, being one of the top salespeople on her team, won a trip to San Destin, Florida, and it happened to be scheduled for that next day. The doctor told us that in the next few days, there was nothing for us to do and we should go on the scheduled vacation to try to keep our mind off things (right). My sweet mother was scheduled to watch our kids while we were gone, and I remember she had a thing about car seats and being nervous to strap them in correctly. She was going to pick the kids up from school and daycare that afternoon, and I had forgotten to meet up with her to strap in the car seats. I called her after I dropped the kids off that morning, and she started the conversation reminding me that I'd forgotten to help put in the seats. I apologized and immediately said something along the lines of, "So, Megan has cancer." Obviously, I couldn't hold my stuff together and had to pull over because I couldn't see, due to something getting into my eyes. Mom knew I wasn't joking, and she began to cry as well. Bless her heart—I know that it wasn't the time or place, but due to time constraints, it was the only option. I remember her saying, "Well, here I am chewing you out, and you have been dealing with that." I loathe giving bad news. Working a lot in sales, I must give it out frequently; however, this was different. So many people have fallen in love with Megan over the years that I have known her. She is a part of our family and loved like one of our own.

So, we went to Florida. Only a few people knew about her diagnosis, and her boss was one. He filled in the rest of the executive team out of New Orleans, and they all happened to be on the trip in Florida. Everyone went out of their way to make sure Megan had a great time. One lady that sticks out in my memory was a VP's wife. She made us laugh until we cried. She was a cancer survivor and chose to live life to the fullest. She told Megan, "You are going to have to fight like hell, but you're gonna win." We hung out on the beach and ate delicious food, and for a couple of days, we were normal.

Going back to reality was tough. The whole ride home was quiet, knowing about what waited for us. About this time, someone special reached out to Megan, Veronica Sparks Waldrop. "Mrs. V" was a wonderful woman who was in Megan's exact place a year before, a young mother diagnosed with breast cancer at an early age. She had young children at home and really helped to put Megan at ease. She told Megan she had kicked cancer's butt and that Megan could too—she just had to keep God first and not give up. This was exactly what Megan needed to hear at this point, me as well, and we are grateful for V being our mentor through this tough time.

A year later as Megan was finishing up radiation, she got a call that Veronica had gone to her doctors and they'd discovered that the cancer had come back and spread throughout her lungs. The doctors gave her a timeline; however, she never let it phase her. She decided to live life to the fullest and inspire others, including Megan, to continue to fight. A couple of months later, we went to V's funeral to celebrate her life. I got a chance to finally shake her husband's hand. Not many men know what it's like to see the woman of your dreams get beat down by the devil and hold her hand, telling her it will be alright when you don't know for sure. This gentleman has suffered what most men would say they have nightmares about—losing the wife you love and having small children to raise, as well as losing the heartbeat of the family. But this guy was a complete gentleman. He hugged Megan and told her, "Even though this happened, that doesn't mean it is going to happen to you. Everything is going to be fine." I haven't spoken to the man since, but I will never forget him and his strength.

After the lull, we were diagnosed with Stage 3-C breast cancer. Now we knew what we were fighting, and the odds were two out of three that she would become cancer-free and live a happy life.

The Great Flood of 2016

> Psalm 32:6—"Therefore let all the faithful pray to you while you may be found; surely the rising of the mighty waters will not reach them."

Megan had her first chemotherapy on a Thursday. Friday morning, it began to rain, and the streets around my house began to start holding water. I remember I had a meeting scheduled with my team at the office and decided to tell them to stay put and that we could talk on Monday. I looked in my backyard, and there were puddles forming. I remember thinking, *Wow, this must be a lot of rain to make it look like this.* Maybe an hour later, my whole backyard and most of my front yard was covered in water.

Part of this story is that we had just bought this house in June, and one of the stipulations we had was that it could not be in a flood zone so we did not have to pay for flood insurance. So, no, we did not have flood insurance...but God.

I put on my rubber boots that all rednecks have on the back porch and stepped off my porch into the water in the backyard. After a few steps, the water reached an inch below the top of my boot. I was thinking that this couldn't be happening, and then it hit like a ton of bricks—my house could flood. Besides the safety of my family, which was the most important thing, my mind was going through the fact that we had just paid our first payment of a three percent down, thirty-year loan on our house and decided against advice not to get the $400 supplemental flood policy. Also, a few weeks before, we were told we had cancer, which had hit the pocketbook.

I remember standing there and feeling as small as an ant and as helpless as an infant. Some people of faith have had this moment before, and they made the same choice I did. I cried out to God to please make it stop. I remember praying, "We can't handle any more; this will break us. Please help." I was walking back to the porch, which now had water on it, and stepped through my back door to get Megan and figure out what we were going to do. We were in no way prepared for this flood, physically or spiritually. She had been watching the news, and they were focusing on our area. The weatherman said this could just be the beginning of a major storm system that was pulling water straight from the Gulf and dumping it in our area—it was going to get worse. I walked back to the back door and sure enough, *What the hell?* I could see puddles of grass in my backyard. By that afternoon, there were only small puddles of water in my yard. God was with us.

There is a drainage ditch behind my house which flows behind the backyard and goes under a main throughway for our town. Rumor has it that there were a couple guys in a big truck driving around who noticed that the culvert was clogged. They decided to hop out and move the debris, which helped the neighborhood start to drain again. They must have done this at the last minute for our houses because our cul-de-sac was spared and most of our street. Eighty percent of our town wasn't so lucky, however. I don't know who these men were, but let's call them what they are, angels.

Flood Aftermath

We dodged the flood, but unfortunately, most of our community did not. They called it "the 500-year flood" because a weather event like that only comes around that often. My father's house, which was built up on piers, flooded. My parent's business flooded. Our church, which had opened as a shelter, eventually flooded as well, and they had to evacuate the evacuees. One of my good friends who lived down the road had to go into his attic with his wife as their house was flooding, and they had to be rescued.

It would have been easy to sit back at this point and focus on chemo and our problems, but not Megan. Megan went out to see if she could get to the grocery store around the corner, and she realized that the church across the street from the grocery store had opened a shelter. When Megan returned, not only did she have supplies for us, but she had food to cook for the shelter as well. I remember saying something along the lines of, "Megan, you just had chemo. You are supposed to rest."

She just replied, "These people are going through a worse time than us. We have to help." I was scratching my head, but you can't argue with that hard head! She also picked up a bag of dog food and asked my daughter Kinley to make little bags for the dogs that had been displaced. It came time for Megan and me to deliver the soup, so we asked the neighbors to watch the kids and rode over. I thought we would drop the food off and head home, but no. Megan wanted to walk around and talk to people. Megan found everyone that had a dog, and she would go talk to them and give them some dog food. I went outside to make a phone call, and next thing I knew, Megan was walking out with a family. The mother was in a great deal of pain as she had just had a surgery and had to wade through the water, getting her belly-level wound infected. They didn't have anything but a couple of kids and a couple of dogs and really looked defeated. Megan had that look in her eye when she was walking up and said, "Baby, I want to take this family to our house so we can help them and let the mother take a shower and clean her wound."

I said, "What!" She said that that could have been us and they really needed help, so we needed to bring them home. I agreed reluctantly, to be honest. Maybe because I am wired as the protector of the house and the idea of bringing strange people into our house with our kids was a bit uncomfortable for me. We brought them in, and I sat with the dad and the kids on the back porch while Megan took care of the mother. The father told me how they'd managed to get out but didn't have time to grab anything. He also said they were very low on gas, so whichever direction they were heading, they needed to find a gas station that still had gas. I told him I had some five-gallon cans with gas in them and that he could have all he needed. He tried to give me money, but I wouldn't let him. The mother came out looking a lot better, and after helping them figure out a route to get to a family member's house, they were on their way. That family could have had a lot worse time. God used Megan to help them. Even when I didn't have the courage, she did not back down from the opportunity to show God's love, and God was with us.

CHAPTER 4
THE DIAGNOSIS

After conferring with a few trusted people in the position to give advice and a little research, we decided to change up our doctors. The original ones were very nice, but when it comes to my baby, she only gets the best! In the oncology world, you get a team of doctors, four to be exact.

We went in to meet with Dr. Zatarain, who was our primary oncologist and our point person for the rest of the team. She said she had discussed Megan's case and results with a panel of oncologists, and they had all determined that Megan was at stage 3-C. This meant that the cancer had spread around to multiple areas but had not gotten into the major organs or bones. Also, the cancer was not hormonal or hereditary, and there was no rhyme or reason why it showed up. It was triple negative, which only occurs in ten percent of breast cancer patients. Because it had spread so quickly and because of her young age, the picture painted was not one of an easy fight. If there was any good news, it was that it wasn't genetic, so we wouldn't have to think about passing the gene on to future generations.

Moreover, this made me so angry. Megan is the picture of health and has never had one issue. She doesn't smoke, and if she orders a drink, she never finishes it. I could go on and on about her healthy habits, physique, and background, but there is no physical or scientific reason for her diagnosis. I believe she was attacked from the spiritual realm. Satan found a chance to dig into our lives and attempt to inflict as much pain as possible.

Soon after, she had another scan, which showed where it had spread to her sternum, which is the breastbone. This took away all the fluffed up 3-C stuff and pushed it over to stage 4.

Do me a favor and never Google "metastatic cancer." It is a term straight from hell, and it is where happiness goes to die. I kept hearing that term thrown around, but I was scared to ask, not because of what the meaning was but because I didn't want to look like I didn't know what I was talking about. I Googled it one night and got very angry. If you find yourself in our situation, stay away from internet searches all together. The computer will give you the worst-case scenario and a soulless explanation you probably still won't understand. Ask your doctor or, better yet, someone that has walked before you in your situation.

Our fight had changed. What we knew about her diagnosis had changed, but what we knew about the fighting had not.

What we knew about the cancer was right there in black ink, literally. I don't remember every word the doctor said, but I do remember her taking out a sheet of white copy paper and writing down every step of Megan's diagnosis. Then, she wrote down every answer to every question we had and literally drew out examples and evidence of what was going on in Megan's body. Dr. Zatarain made us feel like we were her only patients, and I believe that she would have sat there all day answering my questions if Megan hadn't told me to wrap it up.

CHAPTER 5

TREATMENT

Hello, Red Devil

Because of the cancer's aggressive nature, Dr. Zatarain wanted to start chemotherapy right away, even before the mastectomies took place. Because of the types of chemo that would be used, Megan had to have a port put in her chest. A port is a very sexy plastic tube that goes into the upper chest where the nurses can inject poison directly into the flesh in a precise and effective way. It takes a whole separate surgery to get this device put in. This was the first of many hospital visits that year. They had to put Megan under anesthesia to put the port in, and I will never forget when she came out of her sleep. My dad came down to wait with me and was sitting next to the bed. I was standing at the foot of the bed, and Megan began to stir. She looked at Dad and said, "Holy shit! How long have I been out? You are so old now!" She thought she was looking at me.

I said, "Baby, I am right here."

She said, "Oh, thank God!" My dad and I laughed so hard, and the nurses thought we were jerks. Now, she was primed and ready for the "good stuff."

The next week, chemo started, and we had to start with the red devil. If anyone has had an aggressive form of cancer, you are well aware what this is. This is the poison that makes your hair fall out, kills your appetite, and makes you weak and nauseated. This is the bad stuff that literally kills your body. With the right dosage, the goal is to kill the cancer cells and leave enough healthy cells to rebuild your body.

First Chemo

On the way to chemo the first time, she drove, and I rode. She plugged in her phone and put on DJ Snake. I didn't know who that was, but we ended up having a dance party the whole way there for some reason. Why? Because to hell with chemo, I guess.

This is what chemo looks like:

After the waiting room, a nurse walks you back to your station. It has a chair for the patient and a chair for a buddy. The areas are semi-private, but the room is open and has other patients at different stages. For the "red devil" application, a nurse rolls up in a chair with a syringe as long as an ink pen. They literally have to sit there and inject a whole vial of the medicine into the port by hand. Imagine someone sitting directly in front of you with a huge needle, injecting you with poison.

Right now, you are probably thinking about what that would look like. Let me throw in something freaky. What do you think you would do, and what do you think Megan would do? I would nap or watch TV, probably sulk and eat cookies. Megan, however, would pull out her laptop and start calling customers, taking their food orders for work. It blew my mind! I remember one time, she was saying over the phone, "Oh sorry, girl. I can't talk very loud. I am at the hospital...Oh no, I'm okay. I'm just at chemo...No, I don't want you to call someone else. Just give me your damn order." The nurse was like, *Really?* I just laughed and told the nurse that Megan is hardheaded.

The nurse said that Meagan might get sleepy or nauseous or have some side effect and that that was normal. Not Megan—she just sat there pecking away.

Megan would always stay awake at the hospital, but as soon as she would get in the car, she almost always went right to sleep. This was a tricky time because I knew she would wake up nauseated, so I had to focus on driving as to not wake her up. She would usually go home and go straight to the bedroom. I'm sure you have started picking up a theme here. Megan would go to bed, but it was with her laptop. I would express my displeasure with this mindset, but she would always say, "My customers still need their groceries. It's not their problem I had chemo today. And I'm not going to put extra work on someone else." What can you say?

The nurses at the Mary Bird Perkins Medical Center were beyond amazing. It takes a special person to have that career, see the struggle of the fight every day, and keep a smile. Besides the obvious, we never had a bad experience with any staff member. They also had volunteers come by and bring dogs, and sometimes they would give away jewelry. It truly is a special place that I pray we never have to go back to. They also treated the guest of the patient with the same kindness as the patient. Every time we walked into Mary Bird, we never felt gloomy or got an impression from the staff that it was a somber place. The nurses made wholesome relationships with us, and I believe that if Megan walked back in there tomorrow, a handful of them would recognize her and call her by name.

Ring the Bell

It is a tradition at chemotherapy that on your last day, you "ring out" or "ring the bell." On this day, December 22, 2016, we had a great Christmas celebration. After sixteen rounds, she was finally free from the first part of her fight, still smiling. This is a tradition that is widespread, and in this case, it did not symbolize dropping out but celebrating the end. At this point, she had already started growing her hair back out. I will never forget how beautiful she was on that day. I was so proud of her. We went through the chemo process, which at this point, was a milder version toward the end.

When the process was complete and I got my cookie, the nurse made an announcement that they had a bell-ringer. All the available nurses and doctors that were on the floor came over and put their full attention on Megan. She was so embarrassed, but she came out of her shell and rang the bell like a champ. This was the morning of Megan's last day of chemo...

A Hairy Situation

With the red devil, your hair starts to fall out quickly. We knew that Kinley was going to be devastated if Mommy didn't have her princess hair. Megan and I got together to plan for Kinley to cut Megan's hair and try to make it fun. Trying to rationalize with a four-year-old has proven to be quite the contest. I walked Kinley into our bathroom because Mommy had a "surprise." We walked in, and Megan was sitting in the bathtub, holding a pair of scissors. She said, "Mommy needs a little change in her life, and I want to cut my hair. Will you help me?"

Kinley stared for a minute and said, "It's okay, Mommy. You don't need to cut your hair." Megan grimaced and tried to explain to her that she did need to cut her hair, and she grabbed a piece and cut it, saying, "See, it's fun!"

Kinley started to cry and scream, saying, "No, please don't cut your hair! I don't want you to! Don't worry, Mommy. I will *nursery* you." I had not seen Megan really cry until that moment. This broke her heart and Kinley's. The problem was that I knew this was hurting Megan to have to lose her hair as much as it was hurting Kinley. That was a rough night, but once the hair was shaved, Megan looked beautiful. I had always told her to let her hair grow out as I liked her with long her. But that night, seeing her overcome one of the worst parts of the process, she never looked so sexy. She was human and vulnerable, and she needed me to be the man in the relationship.

She did get one of those expensive wigs, but she only wore it for about half a day. Megan decided that she was bald and was going to rock it. We did have a little fun with the wig before she cut her hair though!

Megan's sister Brittney is a wonderful artist and has a specialty for body painting. This is the result of a professional body painter and a bald woman with a sense of humor...

If you look close enough at Megan's head on the right, you will find it hard to believe that the hair is all paint. They went to an event that night, and no one could tell her hair was painted on her head. Since then, I've wanted to get blue jeans painted on my butt and walk around to see if anyone notices. Maybe one day!

If you or an immediate loved one have never had cancer, allow me to give you a little advice. Refrain from using the phrase, "It's just hair." I understand how easy it comes out, and I have even told Megan that phrase, but it's not just hair to a woman. These women don't just lose hair on their head. It's their eyebrows and eyelashes. It's hair everywhere. When you compare it to your life, it is just hair, but to a woman that loses her hair, it's just a constant reminder of a reality she would not mind forgetting.

Radiation: One Hot Body

A month or so after Megan's first surgery, she was doing great. She had her drain tubes taken out, and to be honest, physically, she looked great. If you picture a Barbie, that's how she came out—perfect.

We met with the radiologist and planned how the next few months were going to go. Unfortunately, Megan had to have her implant reduced almost completely in order to not impair the radiation. Because of the spot on her sternum, the radiation oncologist had to strategically design the radiation to shoot the perfect angle to miss the heart and other vital organs.

"Radiation was fun," said no cancer patient ever! The use of ionizing radiation to kill cancer cells is like putting your skin and blood in the microwave. Did Megan have nausea? Yes. Was there extreme fatigue? Yes. Did her chest look like a pink leopard that had spent too much time at the beach? Yes. Did Megan complain? No. Wearing clothes up top was rough at times, especially when she began to peel, and I wish I could say I found delight in rubbing in that cocoa butter, but that didn't work out as I would have hoped!

The silver lining is that radiation wasn't as bad for Megan as chemo. I don't believe I was a bad husband or a bad support, but

I will have to honestly tell you that I never went to Megan's radiation appointments. She made them at her convenience when she could pop-in and get radiated, and then she would leave and get back to work—big surprise.

On the last day of radiation, she got to ring out again. This was another important threshold she needed to cross in order to continue her fight. Shortly after her last radiation, she had another PET scan. Once again, no sign of cancer. God is good. The picture below is an example of Megan's PET scans.

The right side shows her breast when the tumors were active. The left shows after chemo and radiation, where you see no more glow. Her heart is lighting up on the picture to the left because they caught the heart just as it was beating. There are different angles, but this will give you a bit of a picture of what a PET scan looks like.

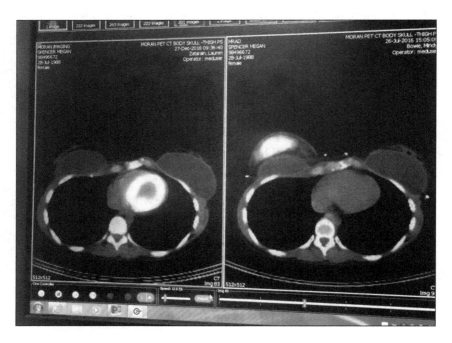

CHAPTER 6

LIFE'S SIDE EFFECTS

M y heart did not want me to put this part in the story, but to encourage and give hope to people in a similar situation, I needed to paint an honest picture. Megan is one of the kindest and most special people I know, but everyone has a point to where they are vulnerable. One of the pieces of advice I received from a very special person in my life who was supporting their spouse through cancer is that chemo is hell. Your loved one is attacked by their own body and given poison to try to kill the cancer. That does not go without consequences, both physically and mentally. The physical part is obvious, but the mental part is not so clear.

In my case, I had a woman who took the world on her shoulders. Megan is a wonderful mother and wife. She takes care of the kids and me at a level that we don't deserve. Take this wonderful woman and give her chemotherapy. As hard as it was, Megan never let us down. Not having any energy for a brief time made her upset and irritable. I was warned of this and would never blame Megan. God knows, I would have been worse. There were times when the littlest things would aggravate her, and I would smile and try to smooth it over. I remember one time, I was sent on a mission to the grocery store. I came home with iodized salt and not kosher salt, and she was so upset you would have thought I caused rain on the weekends.

Also, there's a small thing called "chemo-brain." Chemo-brain is like pregnancy brain, where you forget some simple things and sometimes have trouble remembering. This turned into a small joke between us.

I would never put down my wife, but I am blessed to have been given the advice that this would be a tough time physically and a hard struggle mentally and that I needed to be tough for my wife.

Not a Saint

It was about this time that I went from being scared to angry. I remember being so mad at God and the world that I would be in my car and just scream. It was around this time that my bosses changed my role at the company to a position I did not agree with. In that meeting, after I found out what was going on, I felt like the weight of the world was on my shoulders. It was so obvious that the owner of my company stopped the meeting to ask if I was okay. I said something I regret in a sarcastic tone, along the lines of, "Kinda having a tough time here."

I knew I had to do something different and drinking excessively was not the answer. It was the Fourth of July the last time I overdid it. She asked me that night if I thought it was okay to drink that much. I told her she was crazy and that everyone was having a great time. We didn't speak for a few days after that. When we finally did speak, she told me she didn't want to live like that anymore. Obviously, I was shocked and humbled in the hardest way. Here was my wife with a bald head and no eyebrows fighting cancer, and she would rather live without me. I spoke with my pastor, and Megan met with the pastor's wife. That day, Pastor George and his wife Jill, along with God, saved our marriage. This was a tough time for Megan and me, but we grew through it, fought like hell, and are stronger now.

I am not telling you this to air out our dirty laundry. I am telling you this because we are human. When you are facing a life-changing occurrence like this, you don't automatically straighten up, go to church all the time, and become a better person. It is a fight and a struggle every single day, and although the smaller problems in life don't seem as bad, they pile up if they aren't dealt with. Like I said before, it's the mental and spiritual battles that show up and cause as much pain as the physical.

Everybody is different, and everybody must find their outlet. I made promises to Megan that alcohol was not going to be my outlet for stress; although we still have a glass of wine with dinner or a couple beers while watching the game, it's not what does it for me anymore. What would allow me to relieve stress and deal with anger? I know what most of you men are thinking, and believe it or not, the libido doesn't get stronger while fighting cancer, but that's for another book! I broke the "big guy" code and took up running. It hurt and sucked most of the time, but there was something about going outside and cranking up the jams that did it for me. It did not come naturally for me to just run for no reason. I started with some interval training, and after a couple of months, I was catching on. I will never forget the first time everything just clicked. The next thing I knew, I realized that I had been running for quite a while and did not want or need to stop. I just kept going. It was awesome! I listened to a lot of Christian music, and occasionally, I would break down while running and become overcome with emotion. But that's what I was out there all alone for. When I would get home to Megan, I would usually be in a great mood, and I felt like she was proud of me. My first 5k was an unbelievable experience. The energy that was at the starting line and the encouragement that was displayed from all the participants and spectators was unbelievable. The best part by far was Megan and the kids waiting for me at the finish line. They were proud of me, and, maybe more importantly, I was proud of me.

Covering of a Friend

In culinary school, Megan and I made friends with another couple, Ben and Jeanne. Ben is a genius in the kitchen and one of the best chefs I have had the pleasure of working next to. They have twin children a little younger than Cohen and have grown in a special part of our hearts.

It was a sad day when Megan received a call from Jeanne saying that she was diagnosed with breast cancer as well. It was very new to them, and they were at that scary point when they didn't know what stage or type or what the future held in general. I reached out to Ben via text first. I knew he was scared; I knew exactly how he felt.

Megan was able to walk with Jeanne every step of the way, and a special bond was formed between the two. I have always looked up to Ben, but being able to share our experiences helped us grow together as well. Having a conversation with someone else who has fought cancer can be very different from those whose have not. In our case, we both knew what it was like to stand powerless while the person we loved the most was under attack by a horrible disease. We shared many conversations that I will not elaborate on. We did, however, speak on multiple occasions about our smoking hot wives and their killer bodies. We agree, now that both of our wives have gone through all their treatments, that we both have never been more attracted physically to them. We have both seen our marriages grow in a special way, and we are closer than ever to our spouses.

Management Advice

I do want to take a second and give a shout out to Megan's bosses at Sysco Foods in New Orleans. Her managers collectively told Megan that she did not have to do anything if she didn't want to—they would hold her job for her. If she felt like working, great; if not, great—stay home. They told her all she needed to do was take care of herself and come on back when she was ready. Her teammates offered to help her whenever she needed as well. It is important to know that you don't need to worry about your job while fighting an illness, and Megan and I will be forever grateful. Also, throughout the whole battle, she only missed maybe a total of three weeks because she was literally in surgery or couldn't get out of bed. The year she was diagnosed, her sales went up noticeably. God was with her.

How Can We Help?

I want you to think about something. One week, you have great jobs and a beautiful house that will be yours in twenty-nine years if you pay triple the price after interest. You are knocking out your debt snowball as the "Get out of debt" man says. As you look at your bank account, the tithing is on the top line, and you are continually looking for ways to help. Then, "We have a lot to talk about" happens. What they don't talk about is how great doctors like to get paid for their services, as they should. I would never complain about paying for a doctor, especially if there is a life on the line, but it isn't cheap.

I have made some bad decisions in my life. By deciding to go to graduate school in Florida, I had to take out an obscene amount of student loans to pay the out-of-state tuition. While having a master's degree is great, and it really trained and prepared me to be a great contribution to the professional world, I never really counted the total cost. Now, my wife and I must pay basically an extra house payment to the government for my student loans. What could we be doing now with extra money every month you ask? A lot. These student loans never go away, even if cancer enters your life. They are not bankrupt-able. They follow you around until you pay them, or you die. What really hurts is that Megan is yoked in with me and my choice. If I ever talk to kids in high school or who consider higher education, I look them in the eye and beg them to weigh their choices and do everything they can to get a grant or scholarship.

By the grace of God, Megan works for a great company with great benefits (So as you look for a company to work for, pay attention to the benefits!). I would also like to take a second and endorse health saving accounts or HSA plans. If we had been on an 80/20 plan, we would have been in a huge bind. With the HSA plan, you pay for 100 percent up front until a certain amount, and then health insurance pays for 100 percent. We hit our maximum quickly, and then we were clear. It was a big struggle as Megan was diagnosed in July, so by the time we hit our maximum, it was the end of the year, and we were about to reset the accounts.

I got a call from an old fraternity brother Trey who owns Southern Fundraising, and he asked what we needed regarding financial help. My first reaction was, "Nothing, bro—we don't need anyone's charity." I didn't tell him that, but I told him I would speak to Megan and that we would call him back. This was a "gut-check" moment as we weren't used to being in this position, and we had always worked for what we had. The Bible says to "Owe no man anything, except to love one another..." Romans 13:8

Megan was a little kinder than I was but still caught off guard. I spoke again to my father about the situation as I usually do when I need advice, and I will never forget our conversation.

He said, "Jordan, why do you give?"

I said, "Because I like it—it gives Megan and I a good feeling."

He said, "Do you think that there are people out there that have more money than you?" I said that of course there were. He continued, "People want to give money because they want to help and relate to your family. Some people have cut your grass, and others have brought you meals. They do it because they want to help. Don't take away an opportunity for people to come together for the greater good. If everyone came together to do a little, it <u>will</u> change your life."

Dang it, Dad, I thought. He was right. This was Trey's business and a chance for him to show what he could do, all while providing a service to my family. It was a spiritual transaction between two people. Recently, Trey left his full-time job to do Southern Fundraising full time. Do you think Jesus had His hand in this?

The members of Tau Kappa Epsilon fraternity, Mu Zeta chapter, as well as friends and family all came together for an event, which was wonderful. They raised money for us, as well as another couple that was going through a similar situation, and we will never forget the generosity.

CHAPTER 7

SURGERY

M y wife's beautiful body—that was the first thing I thought of when thinking about the doctors removing my wife's breast. When I pictured my wife coming home after surgery, I pictured mutilated skin and a crater where the breast used to be. But God. The good thing was that we had the best doctors available, as well as the Great Physician.

We got checked in for surgery and put in a staging room where we had to wait for the doctors. While Megan and I were having small talk with our moms, our pastor, George Rodriguez, and a man I highly respect as a spiritual mentor, Asher Einsworth, walked in. The Rock Church in Zachary, Louisiana, always showed up for us. They brought us meals, prayers, and encouragement, and Pastor George showed up to every operation. We will always be grateful for our church.

After a little chit-chat, Pastor George asked if he could pray for Megan. We said, "Of course," and everyone in the room got in a circle and held hands, including Megan. It is important to note that Pastor George did pray for the doctors and nurses; however, he also prayed for a complete healing. That is important because Isaiah 53:5 says, *"But he was pierced for our transgressions, he was crushed for our iniquities; the punishment that brought us peace was on him, and by his wounds we are healed.*" I wish I could say it was more dramatic in that room than a prayer, but we did pray, and then the nurses came to get Megan and take her back. I spent the time in the waiting room having great conversation with Pastor George and the family members and friends that had come out. About an hour later, I got a text to come up to the desk because the doctor wanted to meet with me. This surgery was a two-part operation where the first part was removing the breast and lymph nodes that were infected. The second part was stitching her back up and letting the plastic surgeon do his thing. This was the surgical oncologist that had completed removing the breast, and he wanted to discuss the surgery. I'll never forget—he walked in and said, "Wow, man, she looked great in there. It was nice and clean, and she did great." I could tell he was surprised, but it was nice to hear some "good" news for a change. An hour later, I got a call from the nurse's station again, and I had to go meet with the plastic surgeon. He walked in and said, "Man, the other doctor must have done a great job because she looked great in there." He started giving directions about how to help keep the wound clean and bathing, etc. But in the back of my mind, I was thinking, *Why the hell did you take off my wife's boob if she looked so great!* But you know how it goes.

We spent the night in the hospital and went home the next day. Megan will tell you that one of the worst parts of the experience was the drain tubes. The doctor plugged in these tubes right below the breast, which drained all the excess fluid from the wound. Every few hours, you would have to take the drain and dump the fluid into a cup to be measured and recorded. Then, you had to slide your fingers down the tube to remove all the fluid and particles. This went on for a couple weeks after surgery. The spouse or designated help is supposed to perform this task, but every time I asked Megan if she needed me to do it, she either had already done it or said she would take care of it.

The surgery was on a Thursday, and we went home on Friday. On the following Tuesday, Megan's phone rang around 9:30 pm. It was the surgical oncologist, and he wanted to talk about the surgery. When we looked at the caller ID, we knew it couldn't be good if he was calling this late. He said that while the surgery was going on, he'd removed all the breast tissue and lymph nodes. He had them sent off to a lab to have them tested for cancer. He said he couldn't believe it; the lab couldn't find any trace of cancer anywhere! He just thought that we might want to celebrate because we were way ahead of the odds.

Bald head, tubes, and all, we did celebrate that night. But if you would indulge me, let's go back a few days to the surgery.

- We started the day of surgery, Megan and I, hand-in-hand in prayer.
- Pastor George and our family covered Megan in prayer for complete healing, not just a successful surgery.
- The doctors couldn't believe how good she looked in and after surgery.
- Her recovery was unbelievable, especially how quick she was up and about. She was prescribed some powerful medicine, but for the most part, she stuck to Motrin.
- If the church hadn't brought us dinner, she would have been worried about what to cook.

It is a bold statement, but I am proud to pronounce it; God showed up and removed all cancer from Megan. There is no other way to explain going from grim to great in one day. By His stripes, she was healed. It took God nine months to go from stage four breast cancer to completely cancer-free. To be honest, it took Him a snap of His fingers after one special prayer and our belief in unity that God could completely heal my wife. I encourage you to pray.

While going to church in Murfreesboro, Tennessee, the pastor was teaching on prayer. I took away three main points from his sermon:

- God is crazy about you—if you are having trouble praying, talk to God as a friend in a casual conversation. Absolutely remember who you are talking to, which is the Creator of the heavens and the earth, but keep it light. Tell God how your day is going and what is bothering you. I found myself talking to God in the car about the weather, asking for guidance, and wondering what was going to happen at the game that night. The Bible says to pray without ceasing, and if you believe God is real and is with you, don't you think He can hear you and wants to chat?

- Always look for opportunities to pray—at The Rock Church in Zachary, Louisiana, I bumped into the pastor one day, and he asked how I was. I told him I was a little under the weather and couldn't shake this cold I was facing. He said, "Let me pray for you." He walked up and put his hand on my chest and prayed. It wasn't long and drawn out, but it was effective, and it really left an impression on me. Rewind a few years in Tennessee—the second point in the sermon was to always look for opportunities to pray. Don't be weird about it, but let's say you get to work and your coworker said he or she had the worst night of sleep. That is an opening! You might step in and say the following, "That's terrible; I would like to pray for you." Before your coworker can say anything, pray, "Dear Heavenly Father, give so-and-so the strength to make the best of their day and help give them rest tonight. In Jesus's name, Amen." This will be your "mic drop" moment, or if they are looking at you crazy, just walk away. But you will have made an impression, and the pastor said, "Don't be surprised when they start to look up to you." There was a time Megan was upset with me, and I grabbed her hand and said, "Let's pray." Unfortunately, it did not move mountains but merely drew fire from the heavens.

- Believe what you are praying—in Genesis, God gave Adam, or mankind in general, dominion over all living things on the earth. It is up to us to claim that dominion. We should do so "In Jesus's name."

    o Colossians 3:16-17—*Let the word of Christ dwell richly among you, in all wisdom and teaching and admonishing one another through psalms, hymns, and spiritual songs, singing to God with gratitude in your hearts. And whatever you do, in word or in deed, do everything in the name of the Lord Jesus, giving thanks to God the Father through him.*

    o Acts 3:6—*But Peter said, "I don't have silver or gold, but what I do have, I give you: In the name of Jesus Christ of Nazareth, get up and walk!"*

57

o   Acts 16:16-18—*Once, as we were on our way to prayer, a slave girl met us who had a spirit by which she predicted the future. She made a large profit for her owners by fortune-telling. As she followed Paul and us she cried out, "These men, who are proclaiming to you the way of salvation, are the servants of the most high God." She did this for many days. Paul was greatly annoyed. Turning to the spirit he said, "I command you in the name of Jesus Christ to come out of her!" And it came out right away.*

These are just a few examples of great men acting in a state of dominion and working in Jesus's name. My friend Jesus made a clear suggestion about praying in John 14:13: *"Whatever you ask in my name, I will do it so that the Father may be glorified in the Son."*

CHAPTER 8

FAITH IN FINANCES

"Daddy, will you make me a lemonade stand?" my sweet daughter Kinley asked. We were eating dinner at the table as we do almost every night, and the conversation shifted from the "What was the best part of your day?" conversations as we usually did to money. I'm not exactly sure what Megan and I were talking about, but we usually try not to talk about finances at the dinner table. Kinley broke in and asked the question about me building her a lemonade stand. I thought it was weird she was asking me because Megan is the carpenter in the family, but, of course, I played the dad and said I would. I asked back, "Why do you want a lemonade stand?"

She looked me and said, "So I can help make some money. You and Mommie won't have to worry about money anymore." God was there that day. This five-year-old broke my heart, and I wasn't prepared for it. My parents were excellent providers, and I never felt scared about anything. I looked at her in the eye and lied, telling her that her Mom and Dad had everything under control and we all were just fine. I told her I would build her a lemonade stand if she wanted to make some money to save in her piggy bank to buy something for herself or someone else. My daughter will not be given everything she asks for, but God help me, she will never worry about money if she is in our house.

This is the point that some people reach to where they say that they have had it, and I had reached that point.

The Bible says to not owe people anything but love, and we owed a lot of people more than that. We had started fighting cancer, and it put a huge, metaphorical chain around our neck. Put that chain on top of all the other chains, i.e. having a huge house with a huge mortgage. We didn't want to live like this anymore, but we had cancer, so what could we do? Shortly after this, I sat Megan down, and we had a frank conversation. I asked her, "If our situation turns worse, what would you rather—a big, comfortable house to sit in or would you rather experience things and travel?"

She looked at me and said, "But did you die!" in a crazy, Asian accent like from the movie *The Hangover.* I almost died laughing, but she agreed with what I was feeling that we should try to live to the max and experience as much as we could. We can't decide how long, but we can decide how much—praise God.

God was also there when Megan was in chemo, and she didn't draw the shades and sit in a dark corner, acting like Eeyore from *Winnie the Pooh.* "I'm so sad," never came out of her mouth. If she couldn't get out of bed, she got on the phone. If she couldn't get out in her car, she got on her laptop. When she got onto the more "stable" chemo, it got to the point where she would go to work, drive herself to chemo, and then get back out there. Megan arranged her treatment schedules around her companies' order cut-off to make sure she had time after she was done to get her orders in. Point is, this could have set Megan's career back, but it did not. Do not be mistaken by thinking this was sympathy sales.

She is just that good. As I mentioned before, her sales went up. Megan is a special breed of superhero. I know some of you are scratching your heads, saying either "There is no way" or "Our case is different." Do not be mistaken—she is human, and there were some bad days. Megan had to <u>choose</u> every day to get out of bed. Those bad days following a treatment, she had to <u>choose</u> to get out of bed and come sit at the dinner table, whether she ate or not. After you hear this, I just want to double my age real quick and be that sixty-six-year-old man staring you right in the eye and tell you that eating (which is a spiritual act) with your family every time you are able to is important. Also, thanking the good Lord for the food that you eat is part of the solution.

Faith of A Fisherman

There is a time that will come when you will need to have faith. If you are not exactly sure what faith means, look at Hebrews chapter 11.

Now faith is the reality of what is hoped for, the proof of what is not seen (Heb. 11:1). To generalize, faith is believing in what you cannot see. I want to take a few minutes and look at Peter's recruitment at the Lake of Galilee. It was in the morning when Peter and Andrew were just coming in from fishing all night. I want you to put yourself in Peter's position, even if it means changing the perspective to modern times.

There you are with your brother Andrew, and you got your butts kicked all night, not catching any fish. You have been a fisherman your whole life and have learned that the best time to work is at night. Off in the distance, you see a substantial crowd walking up the beach. As you are working on fixing your nets, you notice it is Jesus who is preaching to a large crowd. You are familiar with Jesus and have a regard for Him, but then He looks over and says, "What's up? Can I stand on your boat to talk to these people?"

Stop right there. What would you say? I've thought about this a lot. I would probably be grumpy and tired. I would probably be thinking about a warm meal and my beautiful wife, not sticking around work to listen to someone preach.

But Peter had faith, and he allowed Jesus to use his boat. Go back into his shoes. A few minutes later, Jesus looks over and says, "So, where's your fish?" I would grumble at this point for sure. Then Jesus say, "Look, let's go around the corner there, and we'll surely catch fish."

At this point, I would say, "Okay, carpenter! What do you know about fishing? Thanks for the advice. Let's go home."

What would you say? Peter basically said, "Sure thing, let's go. I trust you," and their nets couldn't hold all the fish they caught. Jesus then told them to throw the nets down and follow Him and He would make them fishers of men.

It's a little easier to try to seize opportunities if you look. I was in a surgery waiting area waiting for my mother to get out of a surgery one day when I saw an old lady walking out of a con-sultation room crying. She got on her phone and was talking to someone, and I overheard her say that her husband had just been given a grave prognosis and that she didn't know what she was going to do without him. Shortly after, she got off the phone and sat by herself, crying. I felt pulled to walk over and comfort her. I introduced myself and asked her if I could sit with her. I let her tell me why she was crying, and I started telling her about my wife and how God stepped in and showed His mercy. Around that time, her daughter walked out and saw me talking with her mother and gave me a "Who the heck are you?" look. She asked who I was, and the mother said, "I have no idea."

The daughter said, "Come on—let's go."

I felt a little weird for a moment, but I had good intentions. I didn't have much practice dealing with those situations. I will warn you that if you choose to go out of your way to help a stranger, it might not work out as glamorously as you think, but there are always opportunities to make a difference. I think about that lady from time to time. I didn't get a chance to pray with her, but I have prayed for her.

Community Stepping Up

Earlier in the story, I spoke of an event held on Megan and our family's behalf. Later in the year, the community of Zachary, Louisiana, stepped up and came together to have an event for Megan, as well as another great man in the community with a similar fight. It was incredible to see the organization and people that came out to support us. There is something special that happens when a community comes together, and if everyone chips in a little, lives are changed a lot.

A few weeks later, I received a call from one of our dearest family friends, Mrs. Kim, that I needed to swing by her office as she had something for me. When I got there, we talked for a while, and she gave me an envelope. I told her, "Thank you" and hugged her, never looking inside. Down the road, I stopped to get gas, and curiosity took over. I looked inside the envelope, and I was speechless. The money was given by the community, so I am not going to hide the fact that in the envelope, there was approximately $4,500.

At that point, we were in the hole $5,000. You know now that it is easy for me to get overwhelmed by my emotions, and I truly was taken aback. I sent her a message saying that I'm glad I didn't open the envelope in front of her because I would have cried like a baby. She said, "Me too, I would have broken down as well." Shortly after that day, we received another check for $1,000, so that put us $500 ahead going into the next year.

I will never forget the way our community came together to wrap their arms around us. The example they set will be one I will try to follow for the rest of my life.

At this point with the funds we'd received, we had met our out-of-pocket expenses amount for the year with a surgery still on the books. I am here to tell you from the bottom of my soul that if you go into the hospital and owe them nothing, your outlook and attitude changes. Ours did. Megan was a little humbler, but I wasn't.

We walked into that hospital with a sense of confidence that's hard to describe without sounding ridiculous. We sat down at the check-in, and the receptionist said, "Well, it looks like you guys are good to go."

I said, "No, no, no, no, darlin'. We have paid for your services, so go ahead and call the doctor because we don't feel like waiting around this time. Also, when you bring dinner, we don't want the ground loaf, and we want a view."

Most of that isn't true, but I will say our attitude was completely different. We could focus on the surgery and recovery without the *How the hell are we going to pay for this?* in the background. I have often pondered about the amount of money we received at that time. God showed up and used His people to help us. It could have been any amount, but God gave us exactly the amount we needed

65

with a little extra. At this point, we had seen God show up plenty of times, but this time, it was in our finances. I believe that because we were faithful with God's finances, God was faithful with ours.

Make a Difference

After Megan's treatments, we got a letter in the mail that we had been selected by the Jack and Jill Foundation for Late Stage Cancer Patients to win a free trip to Great Wolf Lodge in Dallas, Texas. You must be nominated by a doctor to go on a trip. I thought that was cool that our doctors thought enough of us to try to bless us. The organization rented us a car and covered all expenses for the trip, including gas, food, and a great room. Let me speak plainly when I say that this organization and the trips they sponsor are designed to help make memories with family members who are suffering with late-stage cancer, and we made some incredible memories. Our kids loved it, and it was just the breath of fresh air we needed.

I would recommend this organization to be the source of your generosity if you are in the market for giving. The representatives we worked with were wonderful and made the process very easy. Great Wolf Lodge was wonderful as well. The staff was very nice, the facilities were wonderful, and there was always something going on. For more information and where to give, check out https://jajf.org/

CHAPTER 9

WE CHOOSE TO LIVE LIFE WELL

Life Does Not Have to be a Train Wreck

The legend says that a small-time oil refinery owner named John D. Rockefeller was called to a business meeting to see Cornelius Vanderbilt, the titan of industry of his time. Cornelius was going to try to strong-arm John into a deal to use his railroad to move John's oil. John ended up missing his train for that meeting. Later that day, he found out that the train he was scheduled to be on ran off a bridge and everyone on it had died.

Rockefeller, a devout Christian, knew that God had spared him from the train wreck for a reason, and he knew God was with him. After a few days, he ended up making the trip to meet Vanderbilt with a whole new sense of purpose and spiritual armor. Rockefeller ended up negotiating an even better deal with no fear and became the wealthiest person in America. John Rockefeller's legacy lives on to this day and will for generations to come, simply because he chose to live life not in fear and be submitted to God. This is a wonderful place to be.

Old Testament Joe

One of my top five favorite stories in the Bible is of Old Testament Joseph, starting around Genesis 37. This was a teenage kid that was a shepherd for his fathers' sheep and the youngest of all his brothers. His father Jacob showed favor on him because of his spirit and because he was the oldest son of his favorite wife (That's for another story.)

Joseph was out with his sheep one day and laid down to take a nap. He had a dream that he was standing in beautiful clothes and his brothers were all bowing down to him. He woke up and excitedly told his brothers about his dream, and they all mocked him. They did not like Joseph and plotted to kill him. When it came down to it, they could not but decided instead to sell him into slavery.

He was sent to Potiphar's house as a servant and quickly worked his way up to be the keeper of Potiphar's house. Potiphar had a beautiful wife, and when she laid eyes on Joseph, she wanted to engage in a sexual relationship with him. Joseph quickly declined, which didn't go over well with the wife. She then accused Joseph of trying to come on to her, which didn't go over well with Potiphar. He had Joseph thrown into Pharaoh's political prison, where you were sent for simply disagreeing with Pharaoh or just because. A few years later, Pharaoh had a tough dream, and Joseph was able to translate the story, which gave him favor with Pharaoh and got him a new job as the protector of Egypt, answering only to Pharaoh.

Yes, Jordan, we know the story. Why are you telling us? I am glad you asked because there is a deeper meaning that I cling to in many of life's great obstacles. What if I told you that Joseph, who was the son of Jacob, in which the descendants for all of time would be blessed, was sold into slavery and <u>never once complained</u>? What if I told you that Potiphar was the top general in Egypt, the most powerful nation in the world at the time? That would mean that for years, Joseph was in the room with the top military minds of the time, learning from them. He was a servant, but that kind of education is priceless.

Joseph served not only his master but was faithful to the Lord as well. He could have easily gotten tripped up by Potiphar's wife. He remained faithful to both of his masters, which wasn't the easiest path to take.

When Joseph was sent to Pharaoh's political prison, he wasn't sitting there in a "Life sucks. Eat a doughnut" shirt feeling sorry for himself. He was talking to and being mentored by the greatest political minds of his time and surrounded by great power. If one individual might have said the sky was overcast, Pharaoh could have replied, "No, it's partly sunny. Go to jail and think about it."

If God would have taken Joseph and put him immediately in a position of great power, he probably would have had a tough time. God showed Joseph how to be humble, patient, and wise.

God told Joseph there would be a famine in the land, so Joseph was able to store up food in preparation. Jacob sent his other sons to Egypt to buy food as they were running low, and who did they have to come to? Joseph, who recognized his brothers right away, and before they knew it, his brothers were bowing down to him. But Joseph was not angry or spiteful, and eventually, he embraced his brothers and forgave them. He even moved them close so that he could take care of them.

What is God trying to teach Megan and me? We aren't sure, but what we are sure of is that we are going to remain faithful. Before we bought our last house, we had an offer out on another house. We lost that house on a small contingency, and we were very upset! Two years later, that house, which wasn't in a flood zone, flooded. We would have been in that house with no flood insurance. God has a plan for us, and I believe that if we continue to pray and be faithful, He will continue to steer us along His path.

We Choose

It was a rainy Wednesday night when we left our mid-week church service. The sermon of the night hit me hard, and I don't remember exactly what is was, but it had me excited and feeling an eagerness that I hadn't felt in a while. I was driving, and I remember looking at Megan and saying, "Do you realize what has happened? You were diagnosed with a late-stage cancer, and you kicked its ass. God has you here for a reason."

This conversation might seem harsh or blunt to some people, but that is how we choose to talk to each other, with complete honesty. She looked at me not really surprised but a little relieved. She said, "I know — I have been thinking about that a lot lately. What are we doing?"

I said, "We have to do something." I continued to tell her I wasn't sure what that was yet, and she wasn't either, but we both made a promise that night that we would not be selfish or waste any opportunities — also, that we knew that God had our back and we would try to stay on His course for our lives. This would require a lot of prayer.

Shortly after that night, we decided to go ahead and put our house up for sale. We would downsize and move into a little apartment down the road. As you read before, we'd decided we didn't need a big house and lots of stuff to be happy. This was holding us down from doing what we were supposed to be doing, whatever that was.

Not Yet

After several years of practice, I found my morning routine. I enjoyed waking up early in the morning before everyone else and having my quiet coffee time with the Lord. Usually, I would wake up by 5:15 am, get situated by 5:30, and have quiet time until 6:00. One morning, I was praying to God a typical prayer of this season about what we were supposed to be doing and asking for guidance. In a voice inside of my spirit, I heard the word, "Stay." Being a little shocked at the clarity and obvious direction, I tried to seek confirmation.

I prayed, "Lord, should we sell our house and downsize?"

Again, I heard the distinct voice, "Stay."

I prayed, "Well, You have to tell Megan because she isn't going to be happy with me!" That was a small white lie, although I did have the strange feeling it would be a little difficult to explain to Megan that God was telling us to stay put.

That weekend was Easter, and we had a tradition of hosting an Easter party at our house. We would invite family and friends and set up games, and it was always an event to look forward to. Megan and I talked that evening, and we both were happy that we were staying in our house because of these good times we were having. But God had a plan.

Wisconsin?

My mom's side of the family is from a beautiful postcard town in Door County, Wisconsin, called Sturgeon Bay. This is the type of picturesque town you see in the movies, where everyone is friendly, it's clean, and it's a wonderful place for families.

Megan and I, along with our kids and mothers, all came up to Door County for vacation in July 2018. It was the week of Megan's birthday, so it marked two years since her diagnosis. We had a blast. We went hiking, biking, ate our way up and down the peninsula, and enjoyed a few Old Fashions as well. It was cherry season at the time, so we took the kids to go pick cherries right off the tree, and Megan made the best cherry pie I have ever eaten. Megan and I, on multiple occasions, said how much we would like to move up there.

If you have not realized by now, Megan is a *doer*. On the flight home, she looked up the district sales manager from her company in the area and sent him a random email that if he ever needed anyone in the area to not hesitate to reach out. A few days later, she got a call from the DSM, and he wanted to learn a little more about Megan. When she told me he had called, I got this feeling like *Oh crap, what's going on—we're not going to move to Wisconsin!* It was early in the process and still unlikely, but it was fun to think about the "what ifs?"

It would be easy to look Megan up and realize her accomplishments with Sysco. In New Orleans with no sales experience, she was voted "Rookie of the Year." Also, she was "Marketing Associate of the Year" twice in her flight, and she won the President's Award.

The DSM she spoke to called back not too long after that first conversation and said that he had a position for her in his territory if she was interested. Megan was elated, but this was a huge decision for us. When she told me, she was nervous but kind of excited. I was shocked, not because I didn't think she would qualify or that she wasn't good enough but that this worked out the way it did. It seemed a little too easy.

What do you do when you are the worry warrior that I am? I took it to my prayer time in the morning. It didn't happen right away, but one quiet morning when I was praying about what to do, that same voice came to me and said, "Go."

I said, "Lord, if I am hearing You correctly, You want us to sell our house and move to Wisconsin?"

Again, I heard, "Go." Later that morning when I told Megan, she was excited. We agreed that if God could work it out to where we could go, we should go.

At this point, Megan hadn't gotten back with the DSM in Wisconsin and needed to confirm that there was still an opportunity. She gave him a call and said that she was interested in the position. She explained that we hadn't put our house on the market yet and would need some time but that she was excited about the possibility. Megan's potential new boss was great throughout the process and was very helpful and patient.

The Moving Process

I would love to tell you that the process was easy, but as most Christians know, following God's plan isn't necessarily easy all the time. We were going to be moving away from our whole support system, over 1000 miles from our family and friends—the people that were there for us through the toughest time in our lives. We would be leaving a beautiful house in a beautiful neighborhood with the best neighbors anyone could ask for. In the two and a half years we lived in our house, we formed wonderful relationships with our neighbors, and we will cherish them and their support for the rest of our lives.

Megan had joined a sisterhood of survivors that she had started meeting with regularly to show and receive support. They would encourage each other and, most importantly, have fun together. Megan would come home laughing and in the best mood. Laughter truly is the best medicine.

Let's be honest—moving from Louisiana to Wisconsin is a big change. Moving from Louisiana to Wisconsin in the dead of winter is outrageous. When we were telling people from Louisiana that we were moving to Wisconsin, they all said the same thing: "You do know it's cold there right?" To say it is cold is an understatement of the century!

Before I left, I bought a truck. In the fictional book called *Moving to Wisconsin for Dummies,* I missed the part that having a rear-wheel drive truck with no four-wheel drive is a terrible idea! The house we were moving into was on a hill, so on the wrong day, I might turn west to get to the main road up the hill but end up east down the hill. It hasn't come to that because I am too chicken to drive when the roads are covered with snow or ice.

On the other hand, the people up here have been fantastic. Megan drove off into a ditch thinking it was a driveway once, and immediately, cars started pulling over, and random strangers helped pull Megan out.

We are blessed to have found our new church. They have made our transition a lot easier and more pleasant. The first time we attended, we were downstairs trying to get the kids situated when a very nice man walked up to us and asked if we needed a hand. After a few minutes of pleasantries, I learned that this was the senior pastor and that he'd found out there were visitors and wanted to come down and introduce himself. The church is a fundamental part of our lives, and Sturgeon Bay Community Church has wrapped its arms around us. We are looking forward to having this place to serve.

The Professional

As the man of the house, I am not going to sit here and tell you it has been a completely stress-free transition. For my last job, I was the foodservice manager for a wholesale distributor. I loved it and had the respect of my co-workers, managers, and customers. I believe that when I showed up it mattered and made a difference, and I was paid well to do so. With my network, it should have been easy to find a similar position or even an elevated position. WRONG. I sent out hundreds of resumes and emails. I asked people to send out emails and reference letters on my behalf, and nothing. I thought I had a job lined up with a company before we moved, but when we got here, it was no longer available, for whatever reason. I have a big, fancy degree and experience that should be transferrable over many different industries, but nothing. After approximately a month, I was offered a position to stock shelves at a big box store part-time and would have made around $180 a week. I almost considered it to at least get out of the house. For around seventy days, I was out of work with no prospect of finding a job.

Megan told me on multiple occasions that it would be okay and that God had a plan. After about fifty days, it really hit me hard. There was one night where I could not sleep. The thought crossed my mind, *Would Megan be better off without me?* I quickly dismissed that idea, but it really scared me. I hated the feeling of not being the head of the household but the anchor.

The next day, Megan and I were sitting at the kitchen table, and I told her I wanted to talk to her. I told her, "I know I am sucking at life right now, and I am sorry for holding you down." I did really feel like hell because me not finding a job was hindering us buying a house, as well as the fact that the money we made from the sale of our house was not going to last forever. Also, it is the man's job to provide for his family, and I was not. We talked candidly about what was going on. You know by now that I am married to a high energy, high-achieving superwoman who is incredible at what she does, and not being able to support her in all areas was tough. In general, most of time in the mornings, Megan would ask me what I had planned for the day. "Look for a job" was the obvious answer, and it was usually followed by some laundry or other "house-husband" duties. It's not like I could go outside in the frozen tundra—heck, the dogs didn't even want to go outside. Megan was very gracious and reminded me again that God had a plan and that she loved me. I needed to hear that from her as I believe that we can get through anything together if we stick together. This again was one of those moments where I had to let go and throw it all out there at God's feet.

I believe God was humbling me in a way. I had spent a great deal of time in the past few years working a great job that I loved, but maybe I needed to be brought down a notch.

I would love to say that I did not complain like Joseph. However, now that I am looking back, I realize now more than ever that it was another season in life when being faithful to God was a bit more challenging.

CHAPTER 10

LIFE AFTER CANCER

It has been three years since, "We have a lot to talk about." Since that day, I have had many family and friends either become diagnosed with cancer, continue their fight with cancer, or hear that final calling to heaven. Therefore, we will never say that having cancer was in any way a good thing. I hate cancer. But cancer did not win in our story. Cancer has no place in our lives, and, more importantly, with God's power and mercy, the devil is not welcome in our lives either.

Our Reminder

I looked at my phone after receiving a text from Megan. "The doctor said it's time for a PET scan. Do you think we can handle it?" This was code for, "Can we afford it?" We are on bi-yearly scans now, and the last one we had was in December of last year. It's unfortunate she must ask this question, but I appreciate her inclusion. We only have one bank account. As the Bible says, we are equally yoked. She knows how much money we have/don't have. I told you in previous chapters the plus side of being on a health-care savings plan. The bad side is that up to this point in the year, we have barely scratched our out-of-pocket cost. A PET scan costs a couple thousand dollars that we will be on the hook for. This is the first part of our reminder.

It goes without saying how important these scans are, and missing one is out of the question. I always tell her that whatever it takes to get it done, we will figure out the payments. Hospitals typically don't mind payment plans.

The second part of the reminder of cancer's side effects is fear. What if something shows up on the scan? We just moved our family away from our main support group and our doctors. How could we manage another fight? Even though we know God had His hand in curing Megan and continues to keep her cancer-free, we are still afraid. Then, I get angry because I am afraid, and Megan gets anxious and short-tempered, thinking something has the chance of showing up and knocking her down again. There is approximately a two-week period between the appointment being scheduled and the actual appointment. As I stated in previous chapters, the wait for the results is equally as daunting—the not knowing. Ideally, the doctor could just give a quick call or text and say "We're all clear." That would be fantastic, but they insist on, "You need to come into our office so we can talk about your scan." This results in yet another doctor bill, and the cycle goes on and on.

Megan and I are rebuilding our lives. We have grown stronger together, but there are still scars—physical, mental, and spiritual.

Physical: Thanks to God's grace and great doctors, this one is less obvious. Especially now that we have moved out-of-state, no one can tell that a few years ago, Megan was in chemotherapy fighting cancer. Although the plastic surgeon did a wonderful job reconstructing Megan's body, I continue to say from the bottom of my heart that Megan is the most beautiful woman in the world. Some people might think that a man would lose some of the physical attraction to his wife after undergoing processes like this, but I am not one of those men.

There is still lingering pain that shows up around the breast and in the armpit area. I have made the mistake of trying to tickle her or wrestle around in general, and it did not end well for either of us!

The question of pregnancy is always in the back of our minds, and we talk about it quite often. Would it even be possible? What are the risks? We imagine all kinds of scenarios, but when it comes down to it, we are leaving it in God's hands.

Mental: It's impossible for us to not think about the past and to not worry about the future. We must be careful about what we say around our daughter Kinley as she gets a little anxious when she hears the word "cancer" or when Mommy has any type of doctor's appointment. Unfortunately, she was old enough to develop a negative sensory recall when the subject comes up.

However, we try to intentionally say "yes" to experiences and "no" to stress and things that are not of the kingdom. Saying yes to opportunities has taken us further than we have ever thought possible in the smallest and largest ways, and we have experienced things we never thought of—for example:

- I was told that I would be a good youth leader for the high school and middle school youth group at church. This is WAY out of my comfort zone, and it's not the easiest way to serve in the church. I have always looked up to these leaders because they show up every week on off days at church and always show a positive face. Our church is blessed in the fact that we get kids that not only <u>need</u> to be a part of a youth group but <u>want</u> to be a part of a youth group. A youth leader must be a constant, solid, positive role model every week and even out in the community as you often run into the kids you serve. However, the more I serve there, the more comfortable I have become and the more I enjoy the fellowship. I have only missed one week since I started, and that week, I genuinely missed the students.

- One of my friends from church asked if I wanted to help with the production of a Premier League soccer team's home games. I found myself, as the gentleman called me, the "producer," which meant I sat in the box and switched the camera angles, replays, and controlled the broadcast of the game in general. I loved the pressure and met a whole new group of friends.

- Our worship pastor asked if I wanted to help with praise and worship, and I said yes. I am not musically talented, but I have learned a lot about the production side of the presentation and love it! In my opinion, in any way we can make praise and worship more awesome, we should never hold back or restrain the possibilities. The praise portion of church is a part I always look forward to. Being a part of that team is an honor!

Spiritual: We try our best to live for God. Admittedly, it is far easier to reach out to God when you are in an active state of tragedy. The Bible states, *"Truly I tell you, whoever does not receive the kingdom of God like a little child will never enter it"* (Mark 10:15).

When Megan was fighting for her life and our worlds were flipped upside down, we were on fire for God. We relied on Him to guide our path so much that we were like little children following Him, like in the verse. We prayed together often and at random. Megan went to visit spiritual leaders for prayer and guidance, and I met with pastors and mentors to help me be the best husband, father, and leader of our household.

"You will seek Me and find Me when you search for Me with all your heart" (Jer. 29:13). I can speak for myself when I say that I have cried out to God daily when things were tough. It is exceedingly more difficult to reach out to God for everything when it seems like everything is going well.

Baptism

> *"and this water symbolizes baptism that now saves*
> *you also- not the removal of dirt from the body but*
> *the pledge of a clear conscience toward God. It*
> *saves you by the resurrection of Jesus Christ."* —
> 1 Peter 3:21

September 1, 2019, was the official day that Megan and I were baptized. We've had numerous opportunities to be baptized before, but we finally decided it was the right time to take the plunge. We were both baptized as children but decided to get baptized again as adults for these reasons:

- We wanted to say "thank you" to our Creator for healing Megan from a chronic illness. We also wanted to say "thank you" for the opportunity for a second chance and a much better outlook on the extraordinary world we live in.
- We wanted to, as adults, publicly choose to be Christians and demonstrate that choice.
- We wanted to be cleansed spiritually. We wanted to be washed, made new, and leave our "dirt" in the water.

Throughout history, there have been many different interpretations on baptism, and we're not here to say that any of them are wrong. This was a personal choice for Megan and me. We have had Kinley and Cohen dedicated as babies, and we look forward to them making their choice to be baptized in the future.

Push Through

Some of you are reading this book because you are facing tragedy. Some of you aren't, but maybe you just want to relate to our family and to see what it was like. Not many men can open up about their emotions, and hopefully, if you are a man and unfortunately find yourself in my shoes, you will find comfort and hope after reading this book.

We never lost hope, and Megan never gave up. Our life isn't ordinary anymore. It's not easy, but it is special. Maybe a handful of our friends and co-workers we have met recently since our move even know about Megan having cancer. If we didn't tell them, I don't think any of them would have known.

One of my friends recently made a comment about me having a lot on my plate outside of work and my family. I simply said that we have a lot to be thankful for and would like to give back to our community as much as we can.

Is there a secret to beating cancer? No. But there is a secret to fighting cancer—stay positive. Stay in control of what you can stay in control of. Every case is different, every patient is different, and every spouse is different. I found a passage in the Bible that I clung to during our battle. Matthew 6:25-34 states: *25 Therefore I tell you: Don't worry about your life, what you will eat or what you will drink; or about your body, what you will wear. Isn't life more than food and the body more than clothing?*

26 Consider the birds of the sky: They don't sow or reap or gather into barns, yet your heavenly Father feeds them. Aren't you worth more than they?

27 Can any of you add one moment to his life span by worrying?

28 And why do you worry about clothes? Observe how the wildflowers of the field grow: They don't labor or spin thread.

29 Yet I tell you that not even Solomon in all his splendor was adorned like one of these.

30 If that's how God clothes the grass of the field, which is here today and thrown into the furnace tomorrow, won't he do much more for you — you of little faith?

31 So don't worry, saying, 'What will we eat?' or 'What will we drink?' or 'What will we wear?'

32 For the Gentiles eagerly seek all these things, and your heavenly Father knows that you need them.

33 But seek first the kingdom of God and his righteousness, and all these things will be provided for you.

34 Therefore don't worry about tomorrow, because tomorrow will worry about itself. Each day has enough trouble of its own.

This passage carries weight and has, in a way, carried us. I urge you to use these words in your own lives, and not if but when the opportunity arises, share it with a person who needs to hear it. We are on this earth to serve each other. Who is happier—a grandmother who bakes a cake for her grandchildren or the grandchildren who eat the cake? A chef does not cook for the money—trust me. A chef takes pride in his or her work, especially in the look of a guest's face when enjoying the meal. Is a person who receives a speeding ticket happier than the officer that gives it? Okay, that one is a joke, but consider the point. It is our time to give back and find the real joy in our lives. We love the situation God has created for us and where we are headed physically, mentally, and spiritually. We love living in Door County, Wisconsin. Life is full of miracles. Say yes to the opportunity of your miracle.

The End

ABOUT THE AUTHOR

Jordan Spencer was born and raised in Zachary, Louisiana and was a graduate of Zachary High School. Jordan was a two-sport varsity athlete lettering in baseball and soccer. While in high school, Jordan developed a love for cooking and got his first line cook job at the age of sixteen.

After high school Jordan attended Nicholls State University and received his Bachelor of Science in Culinary Arts. While at Nicholls, Jordan was heavily involved on campus where he became president of his fraternity Tau Kappa Epsilon. Jordan was also involved in the Student Programming Association, Residence Hall Association, he worked in the dorms as an Assistant Hall Director and met his future wife Megan.

After graduation Jordan went to work as the Kitchen Manager at a restaurant in Baton Rouge, Louisiana. At a Mardi Gras Parade Jordan ran in to one of his friends who said she was going to Graduate School at Florida International University. After a brief conversation Jordan decided he would apply and ended up being accepted in the Master's Program of Hospitality and Tourism Management.

A few months later Jordan was on his way to South Florida, leaving his love Megan behind to finish her bachelor's degree at Nicholls State. This absence did make the heart grow fonder.

Jordan was more than happy when Megan decided to move to Fort Lauderdale after graduation to be with him. While sitting on the beach in Hollywood Florida, and after four years of dating, Jordan realized that he did not want to go another day without being married and it was very clear that Megan was the other part of him that made him complete.

In June 2011 Jordan and Megan were married at a plantation home in Lafayette Louisiana. It started to rain right before their outdoor wedding which didn't stop the party at all. The reception carried over to the hotel afterwards and eventually Megan jumped in the pool in her wedding dress which a lot of people quickly followed suite.

After graduation Megan went to work at the Marriott Harbor Beach in Fort Lauderdale and Jordan went to work for one of the largest restaurants in South Florida, Duffy's Sports Grill in North Miami Beach. They worked hard and played hard but soon their adventure will take a small twist in the form of two small shoes that Megan put on Jordans chest to wake him up one morning. They wanted to be the best parents they could, so they decided to move out of Fort Lauderdale and up to Murfreesboro Tennessee to slow down their pace of life. They each got jobs in Nashville Tennessee and enjoyed the outdoor lifestyle and being closer to some family. Kinley Spencer was born on December 1st, 2012 and quickly wrapped her daddy around her little fingers. In Murfreesboro, they were drawn to become members of World Outreach Church.

Eventually they decided to head back to Louisiana to their roots and after a little time they moved to the town of Denham Springs. Cohen Spencer was born February 3rd, 2015 and rounded out the Spencer family. Jordan went to work for Lyons Specialty

Company and Megan went to work for Sysco Foods. They joined The Rock Church in Zachary, Louisiana which would be a decision that would prove to be instrumental in their life and the difficult times to come.

On July 28th, 2016 Megan was told she had breast cancer and because of her age how it had already spread it was aggressive. Eventually we found out it was stage 4 and when the doctor was telling us Megan had cancer, the doctor started to cry when she found out we had 2 small kids at home. The devil did his best to deceive us before the diagnosis, but we serve a God that is bigger.

Now, Megan is cancer free after some extraordinary events and our family has had the pleasure of experiencing the true goodness that is in mankind. Before Megan was diagnosed, Jordan heard the Holy Spirit tell him that a tough time was coming, it had to do with Megan, and he needed them to get through it to get to where God needed them. After Megan was declared cancer free, Jordan heard the voice again and it said they did a good job but there is still more to do.

Jordan and Megan decided to make another move, this time they chose one of the most beautiful places in the world, Door County Wisconsin. This breath of fresh air and slower lifestyle is in alignment with their goals to grow closer as a family, and more importantly grow closer to God. Jordan and Megan found Sturgeon Bay Community Church where they became members, and both became involved in the youth group.

These transitions throughout the story have not been easy but every experience has brought them to the wonderful place they are now, growing stronger every day. All praise to the Lord our God, the Creator of the heavens and the earth, and the Great Physician.

At the end of his life here on earth, Jordan wants to be able to say that he wasn't afraid to try to make himself, his family, and the world better.

CPSIA information can be obtained
at www.ICGtesting.com
Printed in the USA
LVHW060047091219
639120LV00002BA/4/P

9 781545 681510